About this book

Have you ever heard people say "music is the food of love"? or "the dog will have his day"? These expressions, and hundreds more, our language owes to William Shakespeare. Although he wrote his plays four hundred years ago, he wrote for all people and for all time; he wrote for you.

This book tells how Shakespeare, the son of a Stratford glover, decided to make his fortune in London town—among the jostling crowds in the sour-smelling streets. Find out about the Elizabethan theatres, the Globe and the Swan; the rowdy audiences of beer-swilling apprentices, and the lords and ladies in their glorious finery. Read about the plague that used to shut down the theatres and send both actors and audiences scurrying for the safety of the countryside; and, in contrast, about the sparkling show-pieces presented at court before Queen Elizabeth herself.

Shakespeare and his Theatre tells the story of the man who has been called the greatest playwright of all time, of the man who throughout four centuries has given pleasure to millions of people.

Some of the words in *italics* may be new to you. You can look them up in the word list on page 90.

AN EYEWITNESS BOOK

Shakespeare and his Theatre

PHILIPPA STEWART

WAYLAND PUBLISHERS LONDON

More Eyewitness Books

Country Life in the Middle Ages   Penelope Davies
Town Life in the Middle Ages   Penelope Davies
The Printer and his Craft   Helen Wodzicka
The Tudor Family   Ann Mitchell
The Age of Drake   Leonard W. Cowie
The Story of the Wheel   Peter Hames
Newgate to Tyburn   Jane Dorner
Growing Up in the Middle Ages   Penelope Davies
A Victorian Sunday   Jill Hughes
Children of the Industrial Revolution   Penelope Davies
Markets and Fairs   Jane Dorner
Livingstone in Africa   Denis Judd
The Mayflower Pilgrims   Brenda Colloms
The Voyages of Captain Cook   Roger Hart
The Slave Trade   Anne Mountfield
The Glorious Age of Charles II   Helen Wodzicka
Stagecoach and Highwayman   Stephanie McKnight
The Railway Builders   Alistair Barrie
The Firefighters   Anne Mountfield
Ships and Seafarers   Helen Wodzicka
Canals   Jane Dorner
Pirates and Buccaneers   Tilla Brading
The Horseless Carriage   Lord Montagu of Beaulieu
Popular Entertainment   Elizabeth Holt
Sport Through the Ages   Peter Wilson
The History of Medicine   John Roe
Florence Nightingale   Philippa Stewart

Frontispiece: A scene from "Henry IV" showing Falstaff and Prince Hal

SBN 85340 315 5
Copyright © 1973 by
Wayland Publishers Ltd
101 Grays Inn Road London WC1
Filmset by Keyspools Ltd, Golborne, Lancs
Printed by C. Tinling & Co. Ltd, Prescot and London

Contents

564
April 3   Edwardus filius Thoma Shesford

8   Benedicta filia Thoma Flemming

22   Johannes filius william Brooke

26   Gulielmus filius Johannes Shakspere

A Stratford Youth

If Shakespeare was alive today it's certain there would be a lot written about him. We would read reviews of his new plays in the newspapers, articles about his poetry in the literary papers, and gossip about his lovelife and his taste in clothes splashed across the glossy magazines. His views about everything under the sun, from the government to kitchen furniture, would probably appear regularly in the colour supplements. His face would be familiar on television "chat" shows, his voice well-known from radio broadcasts. There would be so much recorded evidence about his life and his opinions that it would not be hard to write about him.

Shakespeare, however, lived some four hundred years ago, in the reign of Queen Elizabeth I, when there was no television, no radio, nor even any newspapers as we know them today. Although he was respected as an important person in his own lifetime, nobody ever thought of writing about him until well after his death. And Shakespeare did not believe in keeping a diary either. So it is largely by luck that the little evidence we have, such as the entry of his birth in the parish register (left, last entry, 26th April, 1564) has survived at all.

And yet, by looking carefully at *contemporary* pictures, by reading contemporary accounts, it is possible to get a good idea of how the boy whose birth is recorded in the Stratford register of 1564 grew up into the man whose portrait (left) appears in the first Folio collection of his plays published in 1623.

SHAKESPEARE'S FAMILY. This drawing is believed to show the house where William Shakespeare was born in 1564, the eldest son of John Shakespeare, a master glover, and his wife Mary, the daughter of a prosperous local landowner. For a time, Shakespeare's father John played an important part in local affairs. In 1568, he even rose to the position of town mayor, or high bailiff as it was then called. But in 1576, when Shakespeare was 12, something went wrong— perhaps there were rumours about his father stealing from the coffers, who knows? Anyway, John Shakespeare was forced to retire from public life, and the Shakespeare family, instead of being prosperous, declined into near-poverty.

SLEEPY TOWN. In the sixteenth century Stratford was a sleepy little market town, just beginning to become aware of the great changes taking place in the outside world—the *Middle Ages*, superstitious and fear-ridden, were giving way to the new age of the *Renaissance*, full of exciting discoveries (the discovery of America, for instance), and new ideas. At first, though, and for a long time, almost the only contact Stratford had with the outside world was provided by pedlars like the one in the picture, who travelled from village to village, selling their wares, and spreading the news.

GRAMMAR SCHOOL. Shakespeare was luckier than most boys of his age—Stratford had one of the best grammar schools in the country. And it was there that Shakespeare went at the age of six or seven, to learn "a little Latin and even less Greek." This was what Shakespeare's fellow playwright Ben Jonson was later to say of his schooling, rather unkindly. Schools then were quite different from those of today. All the various levels had their lessons in the same classroom. It was often rather chaotic, as the picture shows. One boy is being caned with a birch-rod for not knowing his lesson well enough, while on the right other boys are reciting what they have learned. Only boys went to school, not girls.

GLOVES. Shakespeare's father was a master glover, like the man shown at the top of the page, a craftsman with leather and brightly-coloured silk. When Shakespeare left school, he went to help his father make gloves like the ones above. It was fiddly work, cutting the leather to just the right shape, sewing it up in tiny neat stitches, and then doing the embroidery too, if his father allowed him. It is most unlikely that Shakespeare enjoyed the work. But then there was nothing else for him to do in Stratford, and no money to spare for him to continue his schooling.

MAYPOLE. Country life in those days was full of feasts and holidays—Christmas, Hallowe'en, Harvest Festival and, perhaps the most famous of all, May Day. On May Day, all the young people of the district would gather to dance around the Maypole. Each dancer took the end of one strand of ribbon and, as they danced back and forth, the different coloured ribbons twined around the pole into a pattern. It was hot thirsty work, and much good ale was needed to help the dance along. Shakespeare enjoyed the Maypole, and must have got tired of the mean-faced preachers who attacked it, saying "this stinking idol" was the Devil's work.

NATURE LOVER. But one thing Shakespeare surely did enjoy about his work was going out to deliver gloves to households in outlying districts. Shakespeare walked across the fields with the gloves in a parcel under his arm, breathing in the fresh country air, and looking at the trees, the small scurrying animals, and the gentle meandering river. The photograph shows Stratford parish church, and the meadows by the River Avon—a scene probably quite unchanged since Shakespeare's day. Perhaps the beauty of this countryside inspired Shakespeare to write some of his first poems.

COUNTRY DANCES. There was no television then, no cinema to keep people amused. Nor were there any youth clubs where young people could go to meet each other. Instead it was on festive occasions, like May Day for example, that young people got to know each other. Dancing was a very popular pastime. Notice how in the picture there are three boys and only one girl. This is because it was not considered "correct" for well-brought up young ladies to go dancing, whether around the Maypole, or with friends in the woods. However, it was probably on some such occasion that Shakespeare first met Anne Hathaway, who later became his wife.

FALLING IN LOVE. Courting in *Elizabethan* times was very straightforward. In the picture, the man and his wife just get on with raking the hay while the young couple kiss and cuddle in the haystack behind. So you see, that sort of freedom is not really anything new! Anne Hathaway was eight years older than Shakespeare, but she must still have been very beautiful. Soon she and Shakespeare were lovers.

SHOTGUN WEDDING.. But then, to her horror, Anne discovered she was going to have a baby. If she was not to be disgraced in the eyes of all, Shakespeare would have to marry her. And so married they were, in November 1582. The words of the marriage service they are saying in the picture were very similar to those used today: "I, William, take thee, Anne, to my wedded wife, to have and to hold, from this day forward, for better for worse, for richer for poorer, in sickness and in health, to love and to cherish, till death us do part . . ." Anne went to live with the Shakespeare family. In May 1583, a daughter, Susanna, was born. She was followed, in January 1585, by a twin brother and sister, Hamnet and Judith.

MARRIED LIFE. But married life was not all happiness for Shakespeare. His family home was not really large enough to accommodate his wife and three children, as well as his parents and brothers and sisters. Nor were Elizabethan homes easy to run. There was no electricity, no running water. The water had to be fetched from a well outside, often a long way away. If Anne wanted hot water, she had to boil it in a pan over an open fire, as the housewife in the picture is doing. Shakespeare's mother probably welcomed the extra help Anne could give, but Shakespeare soon found the strain of living in such cramped quarters too much.

NAGGING. Anne used to nag Shakespeare about
their lack of money, their cramped surroundings,
and the discomforts they had to suffer. At such times
she probably looked like the woman in the picture,
with sour face and harsh words. In *medieval* times,
they used to have a special punishment for nagging
wives. They would tie them into a stool, and then dip
the stool deep into the river, up and down in the cold
water. It soon cured nagging. But such crude
remedies were dying out by Shakespeare's day, and
Shakespeare had to find another way to escape from
Anne's harsh tongue.

18

HE DROWNS HIS SORROWS. Shakespeare found his way more and more often down to the local *tavern*, hoping to find there the peace he could not find at home. Elizabethan taverns were often noisy and rowdy, and smelly too, with animals and children running back and forth. There were games, music and food, as well as drink. The most popular drinks were ale (a form of beer), sack (a dry wine), and mead (a sweeter drink, made from honey). It was to the tavern, too, that the *strolling players* used to come when they were in town.

THE PLAYERS.   So it was possibly in the Stratford tavern that Shakespeare first saw plays performed. The players would erect a wooden stage at one end of the room, just some boxes with planks laid across them, and there would act out the simple *farces* and *tragedies* suitable for a country audience. The play being acted in the picture was probably very similar to a modern Punch and Judy show, with the audience joining in and taking sides in the argument on stage. And sometimes, too, the players would play out of doors, on the village green or in the market-place.

TARLETON.   One actor Shakespeare almost certainly did see was Richard Tarleton (or Tharlton), who visited Stratford with his company, the Queen's Men, in the summer of 1587. Tarleton was a clown who, with the help of his drum and fife (flute), could make his audience laugh or cry as he willed. The young Shakespeare must have been impressed. Perhaps it was Tarleton who fired his imagination, turned his thoughts towards the theatre as a possible escape route from his domestic troubles.

GOODBYE STRATFORD. There are many tales told about why and how Shakespeare left Stratford. Some people say he was caught stealing a deer on the estates of Sir Thomas Lucy, a powerful local landowner. This used to be an offence punishable by death. The picture above shows Shakespeare being questioned by Sir Thomas. If this story is true, then Shakespeare would have had good reason to leave Stratford, to escape Sir Thomas's anger.

Look at the pictures on the right. Another story tells how Shakespeare left Stratford to take up the post of tutor, to teach the son of another local lord, as in the picture above, and from there made his way to London. It is impossible to know what really happened, or what Shakespeare's real reasons were, since he never kept a diary. It is most likely that he just got thoroughly tired of life at home. Perhaps his imagination was fired by the story of Dick Whittington or the tales told by the travelling players. Anyway, he decided to make for London, as the man in the picture opposite is doing, atop a cart. London in those days was the only place where a man without rank or property could hope to make his fortune.

St Hellom St Andrew St Dunston in the east Althallows Barking Hackney Billonsgate Bridge Gate

24

London Town

The London of Shakespeare's time was an exciting place to be. It was just beginning to expand from an overgrown village into the capital of a thriving country. The town was nothing like as large as the London of today, and occupied only about a square mile. The old medieval town, protected by a wall and gated entrances, was now spreading beyond the gates. But in the picture it is still possible to see fields in the background beyond the houses. The life blood of London was the River Thames. There was only one bridge over it—the old London Bridge. Notice how London Bridge had houses built on it. It stayed like that until it was burned down in the Great Fire of London in 1666. The river was always full of traffic— boat taxis crossing to and fro, with boatmen calling out "Eastward Ho!" and "Westward Ho!" at each turn. It was into the river that the refuse of London was poured, and from the river that Londoners got most of their drinking water. It was the river that gave them prosperity, and contact with the outside world, north, south, east and west. Merchants ships loaded with the new-found riches of the world could sail straight up the river, and bring their treasures home to London, to Queen Elizabeth, and to the lords and ladies of the court. And it was the river, too, that punished many of the criminals—they were chained to the banks below the high tide line, and forced to suffer the washing of three long tides or more.

This was the London that Shakespeare came to, a rich city, thriving as it never had before, and as cruel as it had always been.

THE TOWER. Overshadowing the city was the Tower of London. The Tower was started by William the Conqueror, who wanted a citadel to overawe the city he had conquered in 1066. Succeeding monarchs had continued to add to it. By Shakespeare's time, the Tower was a dreaded place. Very few of the people who were sent there ever came out alive. Londoners had not forgotten the story of the Princes in the Tower who, it was rumoured, had been suffocated there on the orders of their wicked uncle who later became King Richard III. And Queen Elizabeth, following royal tradition, frequently imprisoned people there.

BRIDGE GATE. The Tower was not the only reminder to Londoners of the cruelty of the age in which they lived. Spiked on the top of the gate by London Bridge were the disembodied heads of men who had crossed swords with the law, and lost. The heads were spiked there as a warning to others, and a reminder to play safe and obey the authorities. The heads sometimes stayed there for many years, until all the flesh had been eaten away by crows and the weather, and only the skulls remained, sightless, bleached white by the sun, rattling in the wind.

O Lord, Receive my spirite.

TROUBLED TIMES.   For they were troubled times
that Shakespeare lived in. One of the main causes of
trouble was religion. People not only believed that
their religion was the only right one, they were also
not prepared to tolerate any other religion at all. Most
often the religion of the country was determined by
the religion of the king or queen on the throne at the
time. Those who were not of that religion were
persecuted, tortured, imprisoned or killed. Execution
was a public spectacle, watched as entertainment by
hundreds in the market-place. The hangman at
Tyburn prided himself on being able to cut out the
heart of his victim, and show it bleeding and still
beating to the victim before his eyes closed in death.
Criminals would be *drawn and quartered*, and their
entrails scattered on the ground. And countless men
and women were burned at the stake, their death-
throe cries cutting the air.

THE ARMADA.   But as well as being a cruel place, the London that Shakespeare lived in was also a very exciting place. In 1492 Christopher Columbus, an Italian working for the Spanish crown, had discovered America. England was able to take full advantage of this discovery, since it was the European country closest to the new continent. For many years, Spain and England competed for mastery of the sea, and domination over the trade routes to the new riches in the west. In 1588 England defeated the Spanish Armada sent to destroy the English navy and the English became masters of the sea, free to roam, to steal, and to trade where they wished.

TRADING. The Elizabethan traveller in this picture
has just arrived home after a long journey abroad.
With him he has brought many goods—perhaps
exotic silk and spices from the east, perhaps tobacco
or some other luxury from the newly discovered
continent of America in the west. Every day, merchants like him arrived in London with wondrous
tales of some new land, some new discovery. Riches
were pouring in from all over the world. Londoners
were the first to hear of these great discoveries, and
to profit from them.

COBBLED STREETS. The streets of London were narrow, much narrower than they are today, with rough-hewn cobblestones instead of a smooth tarmac surface. The houses were narrow too, and hung higgledy-piggledy over the street. The houses themselves were sometimes made of wood, sometimes of stone and wood. As you can see from the picture opposite, they had grotesque animals and weird faces carved into the walls. Down the centre of

the street ran a gully, a stinking stream. Often house-wives would open their casement windows to pour their refuse—dirty water and all—down into the stream below. This meant that walking in the streets could be a fairly unpleasant experience. The stench from the gully was overpowering, and the sunlight seldom reached down to the street below. The overhanging houses blocked it out, and trapped in the smells.

NOISE. The streets were noisy, and full of life.
Shops and workshops opened out straight onto the
street. And the noise from them combined with the
cries of hawkers and street traders, the shouts of
children playing, and merchants advertising their
wares. The men in the picture above are making
basins, mugs and plates out of stone. See how they
are chiselling away at great hunks of rock, and
imagine the din that must have made, imagine your
ears aching and throbbing as you walked by. This

34

is how a contemporary of Shakespeare's, Thomas Dekker, described it: "In every street, carts and coaches make such a thundering ... besides hammers are beating in one place, tubs hooping in another, pots clinking in a third . . . Here are porters sweating under burdens, there merchants bearing bags of money."

And, above it all, the cries of *apprentices*, "What lack to you, sir?" at every passing person. London was not a quiet place at all!

CONTRASTS.   Rich and poor, beautiful and ugly,
all walked through the streets of Elizabethan London.
And the contrasts between them were even more
striking then. Queen Elizabeth passing in glorious
procession to attend a wedding, jewels glittering at
her throat, fine lords and ladies at her side, would
have passed such piteous beggars, cripples cringing
in the gutter, as painted by the Flemish artist Pieter
Bruegel in 1568.

And each would not have found the other strange.
Such great contrasts were normal in those days.

PRINTING. One sight that must have intrigued Shakespeare was the printing of books. Printing had been introduced into England just over a hundred years before (in 1476) by William Caxton, and now books were being produced in growing quantities. The picture above shows a contemporary printing press. Can you work out what the different people in the picture are doing?

TOBACCO. Tobacco was introduced into England from America at the end of the sixteenth century, at about the time Shakespeare came to London. Soon tobacco smoking was an accepted habit among the rich and the eccentric, including courtiers like Sir Walter Raleigh. Shakespeare would have seen the special tobacco shops, like the one opposite, where men could go and smoke their white clay pipes. No respectable housewife would let her husband smoke at home as it was considered daring and even sinful.

Necotiana.

STREET MUSICIANS. Music was everywhere in Elizabethan London. Passers-by could hear raucous singing and blowing on cornets pouring from taverns, and in the barbers' shops the scraping-off of beards would often be accompanied by scraping on a lyre. The musicians in the picture were probably paid by some gallant lover to serenade the lady at the window. The lady herself looks quite interested, and indeed flattered, but nobody else seems to be paying much attention. Perhaps this sort of thing happened every day?

ARRIVAL IN LONDON. This was the London then to which William Shakespeare came, a country boy of some 23 years, in the autumn of 1587. No doubt he was confused, at times frightened, by the bustle and strong sensations of the town—its smell, its noise, its cruelty and its vigour. But no doubt he was also inspired by it, as the most exciting city in the world at that time. It was here he came to make his fortune.

From Tavern to Theatre

There is a story that when Shakespeare first came to London, he got a job holding horses' heads outside one of the theatres, while their owners were inside watching the play. It is impossible to know whether or not this story is true. But it seems likely that Shakespeare would automatically be attracted by the theatre, since it was one of the most exciting aspects of Elizabethan life. Players were just beginning to look beyond the medieval religious plays, the *Mysteries* and *Miracle* plays, which had been the main diet of the theatre until the beginning of the sixteenth century. Now the times had changed. Religion was no longer a straightforward affair. More and more people were asking questions not only about religious beliefs, but about science, art and the world in general. The Elizabethans wanted plays which suited their turbulent age. They found them, and the plays tell us much about the times.The plays are exciting, at once both comic and tragic; great discoveries were being made about what could be done with words, how plays could express not just one, but every emotion known to man. Shakespeare was certainly the greatest playwright of his time. But remember that he was not alone. Elizabethan theatre would have been very exciting and worthwhile even without Shakespeare.

INNYARDS. Every Elizabethan inn had an inner courtyard, like the one shown, and it was at first mostly here that plays were performed. The yard was enclosed by upper galleries, two or three rows of corridors overlooking the yard. It was along these galleries that guests made their way to their bedrooms. They made ideal viewpoints from which to watch plays enacted below. The stage itself was usually a platform set up at one end of the innyard. The rest of the yard provided cheap standing space for the *groundlings*. The fixed gallery above the stage was also often used as an acting area.

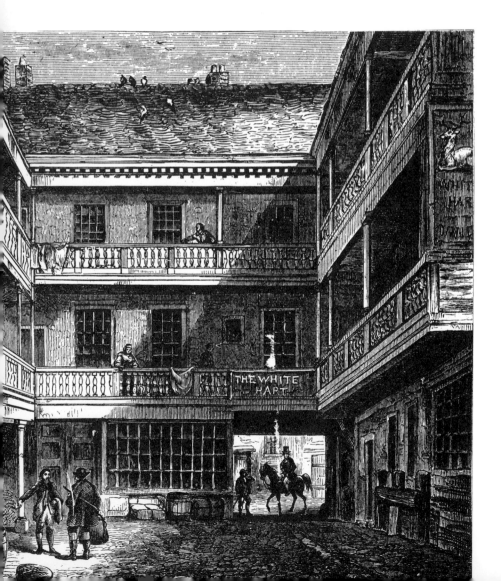

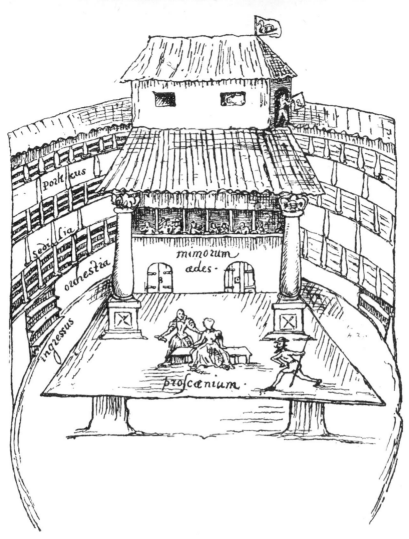

THE SWAN. Gradually theatres began to appear. They were designed entirely for the production of plays. But since the first plays had been performed in innyards, the new theatre buildings often looked like innyards. Indeed, many of them actually were inn-yards converted into theatres. The picture above shows the Swan, one of the earliest and best-known of Elizabethan theatres. Notice the covered circle of gallery seats, and the balcony above the stage. Above that were pulleys and other bits of machinery, which could be used to send stuffed birds, thunderbolts, and so on down to the stage below.

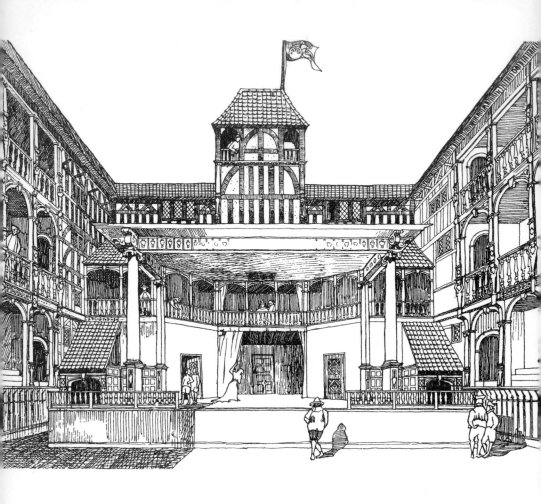

THE FORTUNE. The Fortune Theatre, shown here, was another popular Elizabethan theatre. The gallery seats were used by well-off people who liked a little comfort with their entertainment. The groundlings, the poorest people, the students, the apprentices, would stand in the *pit*, in front of the stage. From there they could throw as many rotten vegetables as they wanted, and shout rude comments if they did not like the play. If it rained, they got wet, but then they were used to that. And as for the nobility, courtiers and the like, they often sat on the stage itself, probably to the annoyance of the people in the pit!

INFORMALITY. People often went to the theatre to meet their friends rather than watch the play. If the plays was dull, as the one in the picture below seems to be, they would chat and laugh together, and not bother to listen to what was happening on the stage at all. And so to keep up their interest, playwrights, including Shakespeare, used to include as many jokes as possible, and litter their plays with comic references to what was happening in the outside world. Jokes were written into even the most serious and sad of tragedies. All Elizabethan plays have some aspects of *slapstick* in them.

ROWDINESS. Most performances of plays took place in the afternoon, when the sun would be bright enough to light the stage. People went to the theatre after their large midday meal when they were feeling quite merry, if not drunk. You can see dinner guests enjoying their meal below. There was usually a plentiful supply of drink flowing too during the course of the play. Elizabethan audiences rarely sat still in their seats and listened earnestly to the play. They liked to take part as much as possible, to join in the choruses, to shout retorts to the actors on the stage—much as today's children do when watching a Punch and Judy show.

ACTORS. Elizabethan actors were a mixed bunch. Acting was not considered a great art as it so often is today. Actors were often thought of as no better than vagabonds. But perhaps strangest of all to us today is that all the parts were played by men. There were no women on the stage at all, no actresses. Usually the female parts were played by younger boys. The fine "lady" in the picture, with her beautiful dress, and ruff, and jewelled hairstyle, was probably a boy of some sixteen years. This explains why, in so many Elizabethan plays, there are elaborate plots about men being disguised as women, and women being disguised as men.

SCENERY. Scenery in the Elizabethan theatre was rather primitive. They did not have all the ropes and pulleys for lowering *backcloths*, the revolving stages and the elaborate *sets* of most modern theatres. Perhaps they had a few tables and chairs to indicate a room, or a shrub in a pot to represent a forest. More often than not, however, they used no *props* at all. The audience was told in writing what the set was supposed to be, such as the "wood near Athens" in the picture on the right. This was enough to suggest green leafy glades.

There were no curtains in front of the stage, which jutted out into the *auditorium*. Therefore all the

changes of scenery were done in full view of the audience. And so, as the actors from one scene carried off their tables and chairs, there would often be an *interlude*—a few minutes of jokes and slapstick; or else a narrator would come on stage and set the scene for the next act, describing for example where it would take place. Sound effects were sometimes achieved in rather interesting ways. For example, if they wanted the sound of thunder, someone would be sent upstairs above the stage to roll a large cannon ball backwards and forwards over the wooden floor, producing very lifelike thunder noises on the stage below.

CHRISTOPHER MARLOWE (1564–93). By far the most talented of Elizabethan playwrights before Shakespeare came on the scene was Christopher Marlowe—a rather puzzling character. His most famous plays were "Tamburlaine," written in 1587, "The Jew of Malta," and "Doctor Faustus," the title page of which is shown on the right. These plays were written in a new, majestic form of *blank verse*, and undoubtedly had a great influence on Shakespeare. Indeed, many people believe that Marlowe in fact wrote all the plays that we call Shakespeare's, though this has never been proved. Not much is known about Marlowe, except that he was almost certainly a spy in the pay of one party or another at Court. There is a great deal of mystery surrounding his death, in 1593. He is supposed to have been knifed to death in a tavern brawl, as the picture above shows. However, when his coffin was

The Tragicall History of the Life and Death

of Doctor FAVSTVS.

With new additions.

Written by *Ch. Marlei,*

Printed at London for *Iohn Wright,* and are to be fold at his
fhop without Newgate. 1628.

---

opened years later, it was found to be empty. Many people believe that he had not been killed. They say that the tavern brawl was a camouflage so that he could escape from England, which was getting too dangerous for him because of his spying activities. He is supposed to have fled to France where, it is rumoured, he wrote Shakespeare's plays.

ROBERT GREENE (1560–92). Another playwright writing at the time Shakespeare first appeared
in London was Robert Greene. You can see him above,
wearing a strange hat. Greene was a well-educated
man, who really wanted to write classical pieces for
select audiences, but was forced to write plays for
popular audiences in order to live. Greene was not
very successful, and he ended his life in poverty and
misery. And, just before he died in September 1592,

he wrote a very bitter *pamphlet* against Shakespeare, saying that he represented the new breed of playwright: "an upstart crow, beautified with our feathers," who thinks he is "the only Shake-scene" in the land. This is one of the first records of Shakespeare's growing success as a playwright—Greene was clearly jealous of his popularity. An illustration from the pamphlet is shown above.

PATRONAGE. The way in which most artists in those days managed to survive was by finding a patron, some rich lord or duke, to whom the artist could *dedicate* his work. The patron would thus gain immortality, and in return would pay for the privilege. Shakespeare's patron, at least to begin with, was the young Earl of Southampton. In return for having some poems dedicated to him, Southampton helped Shakespeare through hard times, clothed him and fed him when necessary, and gave him money when required. It was not only individual artists, poets, painters and playwrights, who had patrons. Acting companies too needed patrons, to help finance them, and to protect them from interference.

The most influential patron of all, of course was Queen Elizabeth, who prided herself on her excellent taste in art and literature. The picture below shows a poet presenting a copy of his latest book to Her Majesty, while in the other picture, the Queen is enjoying the play put on for her special pleasure.

DISAPPROVAL.   Patronage was necessary because
the authorities did not as a rule approve either of the
theatre or of players. Plays were often banned, and
theatres closed down, because they were thought to
be spreading political unrest. The church considered
actors sinful and immoral, and priests made speeches
against them from the pulpit, as shown in the picture.
Fifty years later, under the *Puritans*, all the theatres
were closed down, and actors banned from playing.
To escape the *jurisdiction* of the authorities, theatres
were often built outside the city walls, and thus
beyond the reach of the city's law officers.

THE PLAGUE. But a far more common reason for shutting down theatres was the plague. This was a horrible disease, caused and spread by rats. But people then did not know this, and believed it was the judgment of God on a wicked race. Or else, as one London preacher summed it up: "The cause of plagues is sin, if you look to it well; and the cause of sin are plays; therefore the cause of plagues are plays." The remedies for the plague were based more on superstition than anything else. The pamphlet below is addressed "to those that wear about their necks empoisoned amulets (lucky charms) as a preservative from the plague."

CERTAINE

R V L E S,

DIRECTIONS,

OR ADVERTIS-

MENTS FOR THIS

TIME OF PESTILENTI-

ALL CONTAGION:

WITH

A caueat to thofe that weare about their neckes impoifoned Amulets as a Preferua-tiue from the Plague:

Firft publifhed for the behoofe of the City of *Lon-don,* in the laft vifitation, 1603. And now reprinted for the faid Citie, and all other parts of the Land at this time vifited; by FRANCIS HERING, D. in Phyficke, and Fellow of the Colledge of Phy-fitians in LONDON.

Wherevnto is added certaine Directions, for the poorer fort of people when they fhall be vifited.

16. Num. 47.

And Aaron tooke as Moyfes commanded, and ranne into the midft of the congregation : and behold the plague was begun among the people, and he put on incenfe, and made an atonement for the people.

LONDON,
Printed by WILLIAM IONES.
1 6 2 5.

59

EXODUS. When the plague came, as many people as could afford to would pack up their bags and leave for the country. They hung their coaches with what they hoped were purifying herbs. The picture above shows a family group hurrying away as fast as they can, with the skeletons as gruesome reminders of what fate awaits them if they stay. "Away they trudge," wrote Thomas Dekker, "thick and threefold, some riding, some on foot, some without boots, some in their slippers."

TOURING. The theatres were considered likely breeding places for the plague, since they were usually crowded with people. Besides, the authorities were sure that players were unclean. And so the theatres were usually among the first to be closed down when the plague struck in London. The actors were forced to leave town. Usually they would then go on tour of the provinces, stopping off to give performances in small towns and villages as they passed, like the actors that William Shakespeare saw in Stratford when he was young, or the ones shown in the picture on the right.

The Globe

Not long after Shakespeare came to London, he joined Lord Strange's Men (their patron was called Lord Strange), who were the best of the Elizabethan acting companies. No doubt he started off with a few small walk-on parts, a messenger perhaps, or a servant. And soon he turned his hand to writing, or rather rewriting plays by other people, for presentation by his own company. He would add a few touches here and there to make the audience laugh, a joke or two, a contemporary reference. The first play we know Shakespeare wrote was "Henry VI", a play in three parts, produced at the Rose Theatre by Lord Strange's Men in 1592. It was an immediate success. Within a year, Shakespeare had made a name for himself as a playwright, and had written more plays, including the well-known "Richard III." In 1594 Lord Strange died, and his company had to find another patron. This they did in the Lord Chamberlain, a high official at court. Thus they became the Lord Chamberlain's Men. They found a theatre too, in Shoreditch, on the north side of the River Thames, which was called, literally, The Theatre. When they opened there in the autumn of 1594, Shakespeare was very much an important member of the company — he had a financial share in it—and was becoming well-known for his writing skills. For four years, the Lord Chamberlain's Men stayed at their site in Shoreditch, producing some of Shakespeare's best-known plays. They were very fruitful years. But then, in 1598, the landlord of The Theatre site in Shoreditch made difficulties about allowing the Lord Chamberlain's Men to stay on there. So they had to look for another site, and another theatre.

RICHARD BURBAGE. Richard Burbage whose portrait is shown below was the official head of the Lord Chamberlain's Men. He was a great actor, and many of Shakespeare's most famous characters such as Richard III, or Macbeth, were probably specially planned with him in mind. Richard's father James Burbage had acquired the land on which The Theatre stood way back in 1576, and had built the theatre himself. So his son Richard was extremely indignant when the landlord refused to allow the company to continue playing there.

ACROSS THE THAMES. Stealthily, during the Christmas period of 1598, Burbage and his company, including Shakespeare, enrolled the help of willing workmen to transport The Theatre to another site. They carried it, literally beam by beam, to a new site on Bankside, near the Bear Garden. You can see the new site in the picture, between the trees at the bottom. Luckily for the actors, that December was cold and frosty. As if in answer to their prayers, the river froze solid, so that most of the material could just be carried, slipping and sliding across the ice. By the first week of 1599, it was all done. The Lord Chamberlain's Men had all the materials they needed to build themselves a theatre on their new site on Bankside.

65

THE GLOBE. All through that spring, the workmen toiled overtime to erect the finest theatre London had ever seen. The theatre, called the Globe, was built in the shape of a circle. This gave the players all the intimacy of the old tavern theatres, with the audience on three sides, and a jutting *apron stage*. There was also a curtained recess at the back of the stage, which the actors could use for entries and exits. The traditional galleries were above the stage. The Globe had a fine thatch roof, which kept the theatre warm and the audience dry, but was in fact to prove its undoing fourteen years later when, in 1613, the thatch caught fire and the theatre burned down.

GOLDEN YEARS. So it was at the Globe that the finest of Shakespeare's plays were put on. The audiences flocked nightly to the theatre on the Bankside to hear the Lord Chamberlain's Men perform. The flying of the flag above the theatre meant that a play was about to begin. Shakespeare himself worked very hard, both at writing and acting. The Lord Chamberlain's Men, however, also put on plays by other playwrights, the lost Marlowe for instance, or the up-and-coming Ben Jonson. But it was probably the plays by Master William Shakespeare that drew the greatest crowds.

GOING TO THE THEATRE. Audiences, fine lords
and ladies, prosperous merchants, trouble-seeking
apprentices, bought their tickets for a few pence, and
settled themselves to watch Edward Alleyn and other
members of the company in plays written by
Shakespeare. You can see a ticket for the Globe
above and a picture of Edward Alleyn below. Perhaps
they laughed at the antics of fat Falstaff (right) in
"Henry IV," (first produced in 1598) or cried at the
"star-crossed lovers" in "Romeo and Juliet" (1595).
But one thing is certain—they enjoyed it, and came
back for more. Soon the Lord Chamberlain's Men
were the best-known and most popular of all
Elizabethan acting companies.

PLAYWRIGHT.   Judging by the number of his plays that were produced each year, Shakespeare must have written them very quickly. It is said, for example, that he spent only two weeks writing "The Merry Wives of Windsor" (produced in 1601). It would be romantic to think of Shakespeare scribbling away in a *garret*, alone with his inspiration, as the picture shows. The truth was probably less pretty, but more realistic. It is likely that Shakespeare wrote most of his plays in a small room somewhere at the back of the theatre itself. He would jot down a *draft* form of the play, the *plot* and characters etc. . . . And this draft was then polished up and brought into final shape when he had seen how the actors could cope with it.

INSPIRATION. A great many of the plots for Shakespeare's plays are not new. He did not invent them, but instead adapted stories from other sources, history books, and old legends. One of his greatest sources of stories was Holinshed's *Chronicles* of England, Scotland and Ireland. Shakespeare used it as a basis for many of his plays, including "Henry V," "Richard III," "King Lear," and "Macbeth." This picture comes from the 1578 edition of Holinshed, and shows a typical soldier's camp. Perhaps Shakespeare had this very picture in mind when he was writing scenes about soldiers in "Henry V" for example.

ROYAL FAVOUR. Queen Elizabeth was very impressed with Shakespeare's talent, and the Lord Chamberlain's Men used to perform plays frequently at court, as you can see in the pictures. There is a story that the Queen was so fond of Falstaff, a jolly fat gentleman, who appears in "Henry IV" and "Henry V," that she asked Shakespeare to write a play specially for her, which would show Falstaff in love. Shakespeare did this, and called the play "The Merry Wives of Windsor" (1601) — nobody however has recorded whether the Queen enjoyed this play or not. Presenting plays at court was a great honour for the Lord Chamberlain's Men, but it was also a great chore, since it meant many extra *rehearsals* and special preparations. The costumes had to be that much more lavish, and the make-up that much more perfect, to please the Queen. And elaborate sets had to be designed, since the Queen would not be satisfied with a few words roughly chalked on a board.

JEALOUSY AND STRIFE.   But life was not always easy, neither for Shakespeare, nor for the Lord Chamberlain's Men. In 1599, the year they opened at the Globe, there was an argument between the actors. William Kemp, the company's leading comic actor, left in a terrible huff, saying that his talents were no longer appreciated. He wanted to make a name for himself, and decided to dance all 111 miles from London to Norwich. Apparently he managed to do it, and wrote a book about it, "Kemp's Nine Days' Wonder." The picture above is an illustration from it. Kemp's place in the company was taken by a younger man, Robert Armin. You can see him on the right. It was for Armin that Shakespeare wrote his later *comedies*, where the laughter is never far away from tears.

THE
Hiſtory of the two Maids of More-clacke

VVith the life and ſimple maner of IOHN
in the Hoſpitall.

Played by the Children of the Kings
Maieſties Reuels.

Sam

VVritten by ROBERT ARMIN, ſeruant to the Kings
moſt excellent Maieſtie. K

LONDON,
Printed by *N.O.* for *Thomas Archer,* and is to be ſold at his
ſhop in Popes-head Pallace, 1 6 o 9.

UPRISING. In 1601 the peace of Queen Elizabeth's reign was seriously disturbed. Her favourite at court, the handsome debonair Earl of Essex (below), led a rebellion against her. He was finally executed but, for a long time, England was in a state of secret turmoil, with plots and counterplots. There were earthquakes too, and other unusual happenings. People began to mutter darkly, to whisper and to wonder, suspicion and spies were everywhere. And all this was reflected in the theatre. The cheerfulness of Shakespeare's early plays was changed into doubt.

SUFFERING. Shakespeare too suffered during this time. His son Hamnet died unexpectedly in 1596. And then his father John died too. Shakespeare's plays became more sombre, and he began to write his great tragedies, "Hamlet" (1601), "Othello" (1604), "King Lear" (1605), "Macbeth" (1606). And his comedies, even though they were still funny, now had a certain bite to them. Many consider this the greatest period of Shakespeare's career. The picture, a statue of Shakespeare in a park at Weimar in Germany, shows the poet in a typical pose—sad and brooding, thinking about death and human misery, with the cares of the world heavy on his shoulders.

The Chariott drawne by foure Horses vpon which charret
stood the Coffin conered wth purple Veluett and vpon
that the representation. The Canapy borne hy six Knights.

78

DEATH OF THE QUEEN. And then, in 1603, Queen Elizabeth died, after one of the longest and most remarkable reigns ever known in British history. She had been on the throne for 44 years, and her death marked the passing of an era. The picture above shows her funeral procession wending its way through the streets of London towards Westminster Abbey. Elizabeth was succeeded on the throne by her cousin, King James VI of Scotland, who became King James I of England. James, who is shown opposite, took a particular interest in the arts. He was especially impressed by the Lord Chamberlain's Men. Soon the company changed its name yet again, to become the King's Men. And Shakespeare and his fellow actors were made "gentlemen of the bed-chamber," privileged in theory at least to assist the King in his rising and dressing each morning, and his retiring at night.

_A_
PLEASANT
Con̅ceited Comedie
CALLED,
Loues labors loſt.

As it vvas preſented before her Highnes
this laſt Chriſtmas.

Newly corrected and augmented
By W. Shakeſpere.

Imprinted at London by _W.W_
for _Cutbert Burby._
1598.

THE PRINTED WORD. Printers had no scruples about publishing a play without the playwright's consent, or even his knowledge. And they could then sell the "pirated" version to the general reading public, which was growing in number. The picture below shows a public reading room at the time of James I. The pirate printers would send spies along to a performance, who would sit there pencil in hand, scribbling down the lines as they were spoken. Naturally they could not get it all down perfectly, and many of these pirate versions were terrible distortions of the real play. Finally, Shakespeare had his original plays set in printed form, hoping that people would prefer to buy the real thing when they could. The plays that were separately printed in Shakespeare's lifetime are known as the Quartos, such as this quarto edition of "Love's Labour's Lost," (opposite), published in 1598. But the first full collection of Shakespeare's plays, the Folio, was not published until 1623, seven years after his death.

Twilight in Stratford

In time, as Shakespeare grew older, he longed to return home to Stratford, to his wife and daughters and probably more important, to the peace and quiet of the country. He longed to be away from the intrigues and the complications of living in London. He had fulfilled his ambition to make his fortune in London town. Indeed, his fortune was quite a sizeable one, and he had been able to purchase some land, and also New Place, one of the finest houses in Stratford. The house was set in an acre of land, with two barns and an orchard, and was a *tangible* sign that success had come to Shakespeare. Shakespeare probably retired sometime during the year 1610, when he was 46 years old. This was considered quite old in those days, when people died much younger than they do today. From his retirement in Stratford, Shakespeare continued to write plays, and no doubt made occasional visits to London. But his plays, like "A Winter's Tale" and "The Tempest" (both first produced in 1611) show the influence of the peaceful countryside in which he was living. They are much more gentle than his earlier plays, and have none of that bitterness which marked so many of his great tragedies.

PEACE. Shakespeare's last days were surely peaceful—a comfortable home, beautiful surroundings, his family to look after him instead of landladies in the cheap lodgings he had been used to in London. His daughter Susanna had married a local doctor, Dr. John Hall, and would bring her child round to see him, to dance on her grandfather's knee. There were books to read in the library, memories to feed on of his exciting life in London. And his friends visited him too, to remind him of the glories he had known. But most of all, old age for Shakespeare meant a falling away of the cares and worries and strains of a full and very hard-working life.

DEATH AND BURIAL. Shakespeare died peacefully, some say after a drinking session with his old friend Ben Jonson, in the spring of 1616. He was buried on 25th April, 1616, in the grounds of Holy Trinity Church, Stratford. The inscription on his tomb which is shown below reads:

Good friend, for Jesus's sake forbear
To dig the dust enclosed here.
Blessed be the man who spares these stones,
And cursed be he who moves my bones.

GOOD FREND FOR IESVS SAKE FORBEARE,
TO DIGG THE DVST ENCLOASED HEARE:
BLESE BE Y^E MAN Y^T SPARES THES STONE,
AND CVRST BE HE Y^T MOVES MY BONES.

WILLIAM'S WILL. Shakespeare's will, written a few months before his death, has always caused a certain amount of amusement. For in it he makes all the usual bequests (to his daughter Susanna, for example, he wills all his personal property, New Place, and his other land and houses). But to his wife he leaves only "my second-best bed." Perhaps the bed in the picture which is at present in the Shakespeare Memorial House in Stratford is the one he meant!

IN MEMORIAM. There are hundreds of portraits of Shakespeare, hundreds of busts of him all over the world. But all are unsatisfactory. In this memorial bust (opposite) erected by his prosperous son-in-law in the Stratford parish church, he looks completely wooden. What spark is shown there, to write such glorious verse? But in fact we do not really need a portrait of Shakespeare. All we need to do is to read the plays, or to see them, or to hear them. And then Shakespeare is speaking to us all through the ages.

SHAKESPEARE TODAY. It is over 400 years now since Shakespeare died, yet his plays continue to inspire the world. Many great actors have become famous by playing parts that Shakespeare wrote. The picture on the left, for example, shows the well-known English actor, Sir Lawrence Olivier, as the evil hunchback king in a production of "Richard III." Shakespeare's plays have travelled the world, and are loved wherever they go. The picture below is taken from a production of "The Merchant of Venice," as presented by a university drama club in Japan. Shakespeare is not just an English playwright — he belongs to the whole world.

New Words

Apprentices	Young boys who are learning a trade
Apron stage	A square stage that juts forward in the shape of an apron, with the audience on three of its four sides
Auditorium	Where the audience sits in a theatre
Backcloth	A large painting that hangs down at the back of the stage to indicate where the scene is supposed to be taking place
Blank verse	Poetry that does not rhyme
Chronicle	A historical story, an account of some past event
Comedy	A lighthearted, amusing play
Contemporary	Of the same period; someone living at the same time
Dedicate	To present a work of art in honour of a particular person
Draft	Rough copy of a play, book, or any other document
Drawn and quartered	A punishment for criminals which consisted of pulling out all their insides ("drawing" them) and then cutting them into four pieces ("quartering" them)

Elizabethan	Name given to the period when Queen Elizabeth ruled England (1558–1603), and to the people who lived then
Farce	A coarse, extravagant comedy
Garret	A room on the top floor of a building or built into the roof
Groundlings	Members of the audience who stood in the pit.
Interlude	A short amusing piece which comes between the acts of a play
Jurisdiction	Administration of justice and the territory to which it applies
Medieval	Of the Middle Ages
Middle Ages	A period of history from approximately 450 to 1450 A.D
Miracle Plays	A medieval form of drama based on the lives of the saints
Mystery Plays	A medieval form of drama based on stories from the Bible, both from the Old and the New Testament, which were presented on religious festivals by the tradesmen of the district
Pamphlet	A short essay usually published in a separate booklet
Pit	The ground floor of a theatre
Plot	The story, or chain of incidents, in a play or a book
Props	A short term for "properties," the objects needed by the actors on the stage, e.g. tables, chairs, swords, books
Puritans	A strict religious group that believed that pleasure was wicked. They ruled England from 1648 to 1660, and closed down all the theatres

Rehearsal	A practice performance of a play to make sure that everything is running smoothly
Renaissance	(or rebirth) A period in the 15th and 16th centuries marked by a great revival in both art and science. The end of the Middle Ages
Set	The location of a scene; where the play is supposed to be taking place
Slapstick	An extreme, hysterical form of comedy in which, for example, the actors slip on banana skins, or throw custard pies at each other
Strolling players	A group of actors who toured (strolled) around the country giving performances in each village and town they went through
Tangible	Something which can be detected by touch, something which is definite, clear
Tavern	An inn; what we would now call a pub
Tragedy	A sad play, with an unhappy ending
Tyburn	A place in London (by modern Marble Arch) where public executions traditionally took place

Table of Dates

1476   William Caxton introduces printing into England

1492   Christopher Columbus discovers America

1558   Queen Elizabeth I comes to the throne of England

1564   William Shakespeare is born at Stratford upon Avon (26th April)

1582   Shakespeare marries Anne Hathaway (November)

1587   Shakespeare leaves Stratford to go to London

1592   A particularly bad outbreak of the plague strikes in London

1599   The Lord Chamberlain's Men build the Globe theatre

1601   The Earl of Essex leads an unsuccessful rebellion against Queen Elizabeth

1603   Death of Queen Elizabeth. She is succeeded by her cousin, King James I

1610   Shakespeare retires to Stratford

1613   The Globe Theatre is burned down after its thatch roof catches fire

1616   Death of Shakespeare. He is buried in Stratford on 25th April

1623   Collected Folio edition of Shakespeare's plays is published

More Books

H. M. Burton, *Shakespeare and his Plays* (Methuen Outline series, 1958) —a survey of the Elizabethan theatre and the period in general.

Shakespeare's England (Cassell Caravel, 1964). A comprehensive survey of the background against which Shakespeare lived and worked, for older readers.

The Life and Times of Shakespeare (Hamlyn, Portraits of Greatness series, 1968). A lavishly illustrated look at Elizabethan society, again for older readers.

Charles and Mary Lamb, *Tales from Shakespeare* (Dent Dutton, 1957). The great stories from Shakespeare's plays narrated in an easy to understand way.

Ann Mitchell, *The Tudor Family* (Wayland, 1972). An account of the everyday life of a Tudor family, illustrated with many contemporary pictures.

M. M. Reese, *William Shakespeare* (Edward Arnold, 1963). A fascinating survey of the world in which the poet lived, and the problems he had to face. This is followed by a short introduction to his plays.

Rosemary Sutcliffe, *Brother Dusty Feet* (O.U.P., 1952). An exciting story about a boy who becomes a travelling player.

Index

Picture Credits